Become a Senior Developer

A concise guide to succeeding as a Senior Software Developer

Philip Gannon

Become a Senior Developer

A concise guide to succeeding as a Senior Software Developer

Philip Gannon

© 2024 Philip Gannon

Tweet This Book!

Please help Philip Gannon by spreading the word about this book on Twitter!

The suggested hashtag for this book is #becomeaseniordev.

Find out what other people are saying about the book by clicking on this link to search for this hashtag on Twitter:

#becomeaseniordev

This book is dedicated to my wonderful wife, darling daughter and my stupendous son. Their amazing support and care has given me both the encouragement and time to create this guide for you.

Also By Philip Gannon

Your Dream Developer Job

Contents

1: About the Guide and Author 1

2: Responsibilities of a Senior Developer 3

3: Characteristics of a Successful Senior Developer 7

4: Task Delivery 11

5: Leading Small Teams 15

6: Communication 19

7: Staying Current with Technology 25

8: Outro / Wrapping Up 29

1: About the Guide and Author

About this Guide:

Welcome to "Become a Senior Developer," a concise course designed to guide you through the transition to a senior role in the field of software development.

While technical excellence is a must to become a Senior Developer, there are several other aspects of the role, such as **Leadership**, **Communication** and **Task Management** that often are overlooked. An inability to demonstrate these skills in your work and profile can mean either:

- not getting promoted to Senior Level, or
- not excelling in the role, if you do manage to obtain it.

We'll explore these essential skills and the mindset required to excel in this role. Through a series of short modules, we'll jump into these topics and covering essential pieces of the role; such as navigating conflict, communication with non-technical stakeholders, and how to stay current with new technology.

As we progress, we'll encourage you to reflect on how you can apply these insights in your daily work. Whether it's embracing continuous learning, fostering collaboration, or leading with confidence, our goal is to equip you with the tools and knowledge to thrive in a Senior role.

By the end of this course, you'll have gained new skills allowing you to contribute in a more impactful way to the success of your team and organization.

About the Author:

My name is Philip Gannon, and I work as an Engineering Lead. I've been working as a Software Engineer since 2010, with my experience primarily based in Marketing Automation SaaS Platforms.

About the Guide and Author

I'm accomplished in Cross-functional Team Management, Hiring, Leadership and Mentoring for Developers of all levels, as well as Full-stack Development, Technical R&D and System Design.

I run the SpeakingSoftware podcast and blog, where I educate about SoftSkills for Developers. I also have published a book, "Your Dream Developer Job" which is a guide for how Software Engineers can position themselves as the ideal candidate for the roles that they apply for.

My background is the perfect blend of Technical, SoftSkill and Business Knowledge, and that's what helps the content here stand out above and beyond other content you may see. I'm looking forward to helping you upskill, and advance in your career!

2: Responsibilities of a Senior Developer

Introduction

In this section we'll talk about the responsibilities of a Senior Developer. Here, we will dive into the key expectations and contributions associated with this role. As a Senior Developer, your impact on the business, the team, and the product is incredibly significant; and not just from a technical perspective. Let's get to it!

Understanding Business Needs

Business Acumen

First and foremost, it's crucial to understand that your role exists within a business context. As a Senior, you're role is to provide solutions, not just write code. Every contribution that you make needs to work within the framing of the broader business objectives.

A Senior Developer needs to understand the company's goals, market position, and customer needs. This domain knowledge allows them to align technical actions and decisions with strategic business priorities.

Translating Requirements

Once you understand the business needs, the next step is translating these into technical specifications and actionable tasks. This requires a deep understanding of both the technical and business aspects of the project.

Challenging Requirements

Don't be afraid to challenge and question requirements! As a Senior Developer, it's your responsibility to ensure that requests and proposed solutions are both

feasible and optimal. What a stakeholder will ask for, may not translate into a realistic requirement. Some back-and-forth conversation may be required. Engage in discussions with stakeholders to clarify and refine requirements, ensuring that the final product meets the business goals effectively.

Cross-Functional Collaboration

Collaborating with Product Managers and Designers

Tight collaboration with Product Managers and Designers is crucial. These roles bring in perspectives on user experience, market demands, and product vision. By working closely with them, you can ensure that the technical solutions align with the intended user experience and business objectives.

Working with QA, Compliance and Other Stakeholders

Quality Assurance (QA) is another critical area. Engage proactively with QA teams to understand potential pitfalls and ensure robust testing strategies. Furthermore, interacting with other stakeholders, including customers, can provide valuable insights that shape the product's development.

Compliance, while perhaps not directly involved in a project, will often have hard non-negotiable requirements to ensure technical actions (such as data transfer, storage, access & management, etc.) do not open the company or clients up to Security Vulnerabilities or Legal Liabilities.

Participating in Hiring

Senior Developers can have a strong say on who gets hired on a team, and will be required to participate in hiring/interviewing in order to make sure that new developers that get onboarded will be able to help with the business's goals.

Reviewing CVs/Resumes:

Seniors carefully evaluate candidates' resumes for relevant experience, technical skills, and career progression. They look for indicators of problem-solving abilities, creativity, and continuous learning. Then they make an assessment of their suitability for interviewing.

Conducting Technical Interviews:

Senior Developers can be asked to prepare and ask relevant technical questions that assess the candidate's problem-solving skills and technical knowledge. They may also be involved in creating or scoring practical coding tests in order to evaluate hands-on abilities.

Assessing Candidates' Abilities:

During interviews, they assess both technical competencies and soft skills; such as communication, teamwork, and adaptability. They provide feedback to the hiring team based on the candidate's performance in technical tasks and their alignment with the team's culture and needs.

Mentoring and Guidance

A large part of a Seniors Role is active particpation within the continuous learning and upskilling of junior members. They share lessons learned from their long experience as well as help other team members developer their skillsets to they can maximize their individual impact with the team and it's projects.

Educating Junior Members

This involves educating them on best practices, coding standards, avoiding commonm pitfalls and teaching effective problem-solving techniques. Your experience is invaluable in helping them grow and develop their skills.

Ensuring High Standards of Code Quality

Maintaining a high standard of code quality is essential. Conduct regular code reviews, not just to catch errors, but also to provide constructive feedback that helps team members improve their coding practices. They set and uphold coding guidelines, and expand upon quality by testing adherence with static analysis tools. This makes the review process scalable, and also reduces subjective adherance. They act as champions for best practices to ensure the maintainability and scalability of the codebase.

Organizing Planning and Workshop Sessions

Organize and lead planning and workshop sessions. These sessions are crucial for brainstorming solutions, planning sprints, and aligning the team on the project's direction. Facilitate these discussions to ensure that everyone is on the same page and that the team is working cohesively in lock-step towards common goals and achieving individual and team KPIs.

Sharing Knowledge Resources

Actively share knowledge resources such as articles, books, videos, and other learning materials. This promotes a culture of continuous learning and keeps the team updated with the latest trends and best practices in the industry. Encourage team members to engage with these resources and apply their learnings to their work.

Conclusion

The role of a Senior Developer is both multifaceted and highly impactful. By understanding business needs, translating requirements, collaborating across functions, and mentoring junior team members; you play a pivotal role in driving the success of projects and the growth of your team.

Embrace these responsibilities with a proactive and collaborative mindset, and you will not only advance your career but also contribute significantly to your organization's success!

3: Characteristics of a Successful Senior Developer

Introduction

In this section we'll list out the characteristics, key traits and skills that set top-tier Senior Developers apart. These characteristics contribute significantly to the success of their teams and organizations.

Communication Skills

Bridge Between Business and Technical Teams

Senior Developers serve as a critical bridge between business and technical teams, ensuring that both sides understand each other's needs and constraints. This role involves translating complex technical concepts into language that business stakeholders can understand and vice versa. They can speak Tech, but can also speak Management and Client. They'll often be the go-between or central figure between interested/connected parties and help foster collaboration.

Leadership Abilities

Senior Developers often take on leadership roles, guiding their teams through complex projects. They provide direction, make critical decisions, and inspire their colleagues to achieve high standards. Leadership isn't just about authority; it's about influence, motivation, and creating a positive environment where everyone can do their best work.

Ability to See the Bigger Picture

While they may be specialist in a single area or domain, they always keep the bigger picture in mind. They think beyond immediate tasks, and consider opportunity at a mid-long term scale. Prioritizing maintenance tasks in tandem with delivering features can provide massive boons to the overall project lifetime.

Full Stack / E2E Thinking

They understand the full stack of the technology they work with, from front-end interfaces to back-end services. That doesn't mean they are seasoned Full-stack developers, but it does mean they 'get' how it all fits together.

This comprehensive view enables them to make informed decisions that enhance the overall system's functionality and performance. Even if they are working on only 1 single part of a system, they see how that fits in the entire flow and optimize their work to fit in to the other components of the system in an rational, harmonious way.

Ability to Make Trade-offs

They are skilled at making trade-offs, knowing when to prioritize short-term wins versus long-term gains. They understand that sometimes it's necessary to sacrifice a small battle to win the larger war, balancing managing technical debt with immediate business needs. In layman's terms: "It's about playing chess; and not checkers!".

Embrace Change

Always Looking for New/Better Ways to Do Things

A successful Senior Developer embraces change and is always on the lookout for new and better ways to do things. They stay updated with the latest industry innovations and technologies, continuously improving their workflows and techniques.

Integrating AI into Their Workflow

In today's rapidly evolving tech landscape, integrating AI into their workflow is effectively mandatory. Senior Developers leverage AI tools to optimize coding practices, automate repetitive tasks, assist with Technical writing, and enhance decision-making processes.

Area of Specialty

Deep Knowledge on a single area of Focus

Successful Senior Developers usually have a deep area of specialty. They possess in-depth knowledge and expertise in their chosen domain, and this specialization allows them to tackle more complex problems with confidence and precision.

These speciality domains are typically harder problem domains in which they have acquired significant experience. Examples can include items like:

Performance Optimization and Scalability

Ensuring that applications run efficiently and can scale effectively to meet user demands. They have a strong grasp of concurrency, parallelism, and asynchronous programming, which are crucial for developing high-performance, responsive applications.

Authentication and Authorization

They are knowledgeable in authentication and authorization, ensuring that systems are secure and that user access is properly managed.

Component and Module reuse and delivery

Many Senior Developers excel and creating and maintaining ecosystems of libraries and toolsets in order to empower other development teams to deliver. This can include building, publishing and coordinating usage of reusable libraries and modules via module federation, custom package manager feeds, etc.

Conclusion

In summary, a successful Senior Developer possesses strong communication skills, leadership abilities, and a holistic view of the system(s) that constitute the projects portfolio of their team. They embrace change, continuously seek improvements, and integrate cutting-edge technologies like AI into their workflows. Their deep specialization and ability to tackle complex problems make them invaluable to their teams and organizations.

By cultivating these characteristics, you can elevate your career and make a significant impact in your role and field.

4: Task Delivery

Introduction

This section on Task Delivery covers key aspects of planning and estimating projects, prioritizing tasks, managing dependencies in a team environment, and covering advice for impactful RFCs or specifications.

Planning and Estimating Projects

Planning Projects

Effective planning is the cornerstone of successful task delivery. As a Senior Developer, you need to ensure that your project's tasks are well-organized from the outset. Project Management is a separate function with it's own specialized role. However Senior Developers are expected to aid that strategic role from a tactical point-of-view. They can do so via:

- Confirm Objectives: Start by clarifying and confirming the project's objectives. Understand what the end goal is and what success looks like. This helps in aligning the team, tasks and for setting the direction for the project.
- Break Down Tasks: Decompose the project into smaller, manageable technical tasks. This makes it easier to estimate time and resources, and helps in identifying potential risks early on.
- Solidify milestones: Develop a project outline with the PM to work out deliverable milestones. This helps in tracking progress, and encourages feedback loops by delivering frequently.

Estimating Projects

Accurate estimation is critical for setting realistic expectations and ensuring timely delivery.

- Use Historical Data: Where possible, leverage historical data from previous projects to inform your estimates. Look at similar tasks and consider how long they took and what challenges were encountered.
- Consult the Team: Engage with your team to gather input on time estimates. Collaborative estimation sessions, or workshopping tools like planning poker, can provide more accurate and balanced estimates.
- Account for Uncertainty: Always include a buffer for unforeseen challenges and changes. It's better to under-promise and over-deliver than the reverse. Your team may have a policy of multiplying real estimates by a factor of x1.5, x2 or even x3 depending on task complexity or uncertainty.
- Estimating with the implementor(s) in mind: Senior Developers know that not all devs are of the same level, and some will be able to complete certain tasks faster than others, depending on their experience and problem familiarity. A task that might take a Senior Developer 2 days may take a capable junior 1 or 2 weeks. They know how to estimate for the average level of the implementors, and not themselves.

Prioritizing Tasks and Managing Dependencies

Prioritizing Tasks

Prioritizing tasks effectively ensures that the most critical work gets done first, aligning with business goals and project timelines. While there may be agreed deliverables with clients, there are often inescapable, technical tasks that were not factored in that the Senior Dev needs to ensure happens. For example, coding up a new Rest API may not take long, but there can be DevOps tasks re: IAC implementation, Accessing/Zoning in the Virtual Network, registry with API Management Gateway, etc. These types of tasks are unknowns to the product team, but add additional time and complexity to the project.

- Assess Impact and Urgency: Evaluate tasks based on their impact, what other tasks they can unblock. Focus on tasks that move the project forward and that open up parallel work as much as possible. For example: Making the frontend based on wireframes when the backend datamodel hasn't been defined can lead to significant issues later on. Therefore, creating a datamodel and mock api responses and then circulating it to Design and Frontend means they can action in lock-step with Backend, instead of waiting for an implementation to work against.

- Balance Short-Term and Long-Term Goals: Ensure that your prioritization strikes a balance between quick wins and long-term objectives. This helps in maintaining momentum. If a project is 6 months long, it's reasonable to expect that something needs to be demo'ed before the 6-month mark. Building and delivering incrementally means keeping stakeholder trust/buy-in while moving forward.
- Communicate Priorities Clearly: Make sure the entire team, including stakeholders, understands the priority order. Clear communication helps in aligning efforts and dealing with any issues or speed-bumps that arise.

Writing Detailed RFCs or Specs

Importance of RFCs/Specs

Request for Comments (RFCs) or specifications are essential for documenting project tasks and ensuring everyone is on the same page.

- Clarity and Detail: A well-written RFC or Technical Specification provides clear and detailed information about the project tasks. It should cover the what, why, and how of the project. Dependencies should be clearly listed, as well as scope and risks.
- Facilitates Communication: RFCs and Tech Specs serve as a communication tool between developers, stakeholders, and other teams. They help in setting expectations and providing a reference throughout the project lifecycle.
- Documents like these are "living" documents, and not just one-and-done deliverables. The team needs to constantly refer to these AND update them as the progress moves towards completion.

How to Write Effective RFCs/Specs

Rather than give you a 1:1 template (there are many free ones online), I'd like to tell you what makes a great technical document.

- Define the Boundaries: Start with a clear statement of the problem it addresses and the goals of the proposed solution. It's important to define what is *and what isn't* in scope.

- Provide Context and Background: Include any relevant background information and context that the reader needs to understand the task fully. Reference Other Documents, Tickets, etc. as required.
- Outline the Solution: Describe the proposed solution in detail. Include diagrams, flowcharts, or any other visual aids that can help in illustrating complex ideas.
- List Requirements and Constraints: Clearly specify all requirements and constraints. This includes functional requirements, non-functional requirements, and any technical, business or legal constraints.
- Detail the Implementation Plan: Provide a step-by-step implementation plan. This should include timelines & milestones.
- Review and Iterate: Before finalizing the RFC or spec, review it with your team and stakeholders. Gather feedback and make necessary revisions to ensure it is comprehensive and clear.

Conclusion

Effective task delivery for Senior Developers involves meticulous planning and estimating, strategic prioritization and dependency management, and detailed documentation through RFCs and specs. By mastering these areas, you can ensure that your projects are well-organized, aligned with business goals, and delivered on time.

5: Leading Small Teams

Introduction

In this section, we'll discuss leading small teams for Senior Developers. Not only are you responsible for your technical contributions, but also for guiding and managing your team effectively. Here we'll discuss key aspects of task delegation, mentoring and guidance, and conflict resolution.

Task Delegation and Verifying Completeness

Task Delegation

Delegating tasks effectively is crucial for maximizing your team's productivity and ensuring that everyone contributes to the project.

- Assess Skills and Strengths: Understand the strengths, skills, and interests of each team member.
- Delegate tasks that align with their capabilities and provide opportunities for growth.
    - Match Tasks to Skills: Help team members choose tasks that align with their strengths and career goals. This ensures that they are engaged and motivated.
    - Encourage Challenging Tasks: Encourage team members to take on challenging tasks that push their boundaries. Provide support and guidance to help them succeed.
- Set Clear Expectations: When delegating tasks, provide clear instructions and define the expected outcomes. Ensure that each team member knows what is expected of them and the timeline for completion. Encourage them to communicate if they are stuck, or if they won't reach deadlines without assistance.

- Provide Resources and Support: Make sure that your team has the necessary resources and support to complete their tasks. This includes access to tools, documentation, and your availability for guidance.
    - Your availability is a key component. Many Senior Devs proclaim "They know that they can always come to me if they need help" but then are surprised when junior's aren't able to complete their tasks. Seniors should schedule regular time to check-in with Juniors on tasks, and bring your help and support directly to them.

Verifying Completeness

Ensuring that tasks are completed accurately and on time is essential for maintaining project momentum.

- Regular Check-ins: Schedule regular check-ins to monitor progress and address any issues that arise. This helps in keeping the team on track and provides an opportunity for feedback.
- Review Deliverables: Verify the completeness of tasks by reviewing deliverables against the set expectations. Ensure that the work meets the quality standards and compliance requirements. Ensure all Acceptance Criteria are at least met, if not exceeded.
- Provide Feedback: Give constructive feedback on completed tasks. Highlight what was done well and suggest improvements where necessary. This helps in continuous improvement and skill development.

Mentoring and Guidance

Code Reviews / PRs

Code reviews and pull requests (PRs) are critical for maintaining code quality and facilitating learning.

- Conduct Thorough Reviews: Take the time to conduct thorough code reviews. Look for code quality, adherence to standards, and potential issues. Provide detailed feedback that helps team members improve their coding practices.

- Keep a list of repeat offences in order to help guide them on their weaknesses, so they can break through their struggles.
- Automate review aspects were possible. Not only does this save tremendous amounts of valuable Senior Developer time, but also makes the review less subjective, reducing potential conflict that may occur.
- Encourage Peer Reviews: Encourage team members to review each other's code. This promotes knowledge sharing and helps in identifying issues that might be overlooked.

Pair Programming

Pair programming is an extremely effective way to enhance collaboration and learning.

- Facilitate Pair Programming Sessions: Encourage the team to self-organize regular pair programming sessions. This helps in sharing knowledge, improving code quality, and fostering teamwork. Regular sessions
- Balance Pairs: Pair experienced developers with less experienced ones. This mentorship approach accelerates learning and skill development.

Conflict Resolution

Addressing Conflicts

Conflicts are inevitable in any team environment. Handling them effectively is crucial for maintaining a positive and productive atmosphere.

- Identify Conflicts Early: Be proactive in identifying conflicts before they escalate. Pay attention to signs of tension or disagreement within the team.
- Listen to All Parties: When a conflict arises, listen to all parties involved. Understand their perspectives and the root causes of the conflict. Often just feeling heard means instigators feel more at ease.
- Facilitate Open Communication: Encourage open and honest communication. Create a safe space where team members feel comfortable expressing their concerns - without fear of penalisation or retribution.

- Seek Collaborative Solutions: Work with the team to find collaborative solutions. Aim for a resolution that addresses the concerns of all parties and promotes team cohesion. Often there is a "middle path" neither side considers as their so focused on their own point-of-view.
- Follow Up: After resolving a conflict, follow up to ensure that the solution is effective and that the team is moving forward positively.
- Escalate if required: Sometimes conflict goes beyond coding strategies or engineering patterns. A Senior Dev knows that sometimes conversations and arguments need to be escalated to their manager, or even to HR depending on the severity and content of those conversations.

  - It's often better to escalate something than to presume there is not need and then open up the company to some for of liability.

Conclusion

Leading small teams as a Senior Developer involves effective task delegation, thorough verification of task completion, mentoring and guiding team members, and resolving conflicts constructively. By mastering these skills, you can create a collaborative, productive, and positive team environment that drives success.

6: Communication

Introduction

Effective communication is a crucial skill that enhances your ability to lead, collaborate, and deliver successful projects. In this section, we will discuss how to communicate and present to both technical and non-technical audiences, cross-functional collaboration, and the importance of writing technical documentation, help guides, and release notes.

Communicating with Technical and Non-Technical Audiences

Technical Audiences

Communicating with technical audiences, such as developers, engineers, and IT professionals, requires clarity and precision.

- Use Technical Jargon Appropriately: Use industry-specific terminology that your audience is familiar with. This ensures that your communication is efficient and that your audience understands the specifics of your message.
    - Align on generic nomenclature: A Service, API, or Module may mean very different things in different contexts.
- Focus on Details: Provide detailed explanations and technical depth when necessary. Technical audiences appreciate thoroughness and detailed problem-solving approaches.
- Share Code and Technical Diagrams: When explaining complex concepts, use code snippets, psuedocode, diagrams, and flowcharts. Visual aids can help in conveying complex technical information more clearly.

Non-Technical Audiences

Communicating with non-technical audiences, such as business stakeholders, product managers, and clients, requires a different approach.

- Simplify Complex Concepts: Break down complex technical concepts into simple, understandable terms. Avoid using technical jargon that might confuse non-technical audiences. If technical terms are required, pick-and-choose keywords that will have meaning for them.
- Focus on Business Impact: Emphasize the business impact of technical decisions. Explain how technical aspects align with business goals, increase revenue/opportunity or decrease expenses.
- Use Analogies and Examples: Use analogies and real-world examples to make technical concepts more relatable. This helps non-technical audiences grasp the essence of what you are communicating.

Cross-Functional Collaboration

Full Stack Development

As a Senior Developer, you often need to collaborate across the full stack. This involves working with DevOps, Database, Back-end, Front-end developers and more to ensure seamless integration and functionality.

- Align Goals and Expectations: Regularly communicate with your full stack team to align goals and set clear expectations. This helps in maintaining a cohesive development process.
- Unblock as quick as possible: Never have a team or function waiting on another to do a task. Step in to accelerate unblocking so that separate functions can work as parallel as possible.
- Share Knowledge and Best Practices: Facilitate knowledge sharing sessions to discuss best practices and latest technologies. This fosters a collaborative learning environment.

Product Management

Collaboration with product managers is essential for aligning technical solutions with business objectives.

- Regular Updates and Feedback: Provide regular updates on project progress and gather feedback from product managers. This ensures that the project stays on track and meets business needs.
- Understand Product Vision: Take the time to understand the product vision and roadmap. This helps in making informed technical decisions that support the overall product strategy.

Design and UX/UI

Working closely with design and UX/UI teams ensures that the technical implementation supports the desired user experience.

- Collaborate Early and Often: Involve design and UX/UI teams early in the development process. Regular collaboration helps in aligning technical solutions with design goals.
- Balance Aesthetics and Functionality: Work together to find a balance between aesthetics and functionality. Ensure that the technical implementation does not compromise the user experience, not spurious design decisions unnecessarily increase scope of the implementation.

Sales and Internal Stakeholders

Effective communication with sales teams and internal stakeholders ensures that technical solutions meet market demands and business requirements.

- Gather Requirements and Feedback: Engage with sales teams to understand customer needs and gather feedback. This helps in tailoring technical solutions to meet market demands.
- Communicate Value Propositions: Clearly articulate the value propositions of technical features to internal stakeholders. This helps in gaining their support and buy-in.

Clients

Communicating with clients effectively is crucial for managing expectations and building strong relationships.

- Involve them in deliverable feedback loops. Requiring feedback and comments as the project progresses ensures the final deliverable hits the mark.
- Manage Expectations: Set realistic expectations and communicate any changes or delays promptly. This helps in building trust and maintaining client satisfaction.

Writing Technical Documentation, Help Guides, and Release Notes

Technical Documentation

Clear and comprehensive technical documentation is essential for the successful implementation and maintenance of projects.

- Detailed and Structured: Write comprehensive documentation that covers all aspects of the project. Internal wikis, ticketing systems and doc repos, like SharePoint, are invaluable if used correctly and continuously!
- Include Code Examples: Provide code examples to illustrate key concepts and functionalities. This helps in making the documentation more practical and useful for developers.

Help Guides

Help guides assist users in understanding and using your software effectively.

- User-Friendly Language: Use simple and user-friendly language in help guides. Avoid technical jargon that might confuse users.
- Step-by-Step Instructions: Provide step-by-step instructions with screenshots, diagrams or even short screencasts. This helps users follow along easily and understand the process.

Release Notes

Release notes inform users and the team about new features, improvements, and bug fixes in each software release.

- Concise and Clear: Write concise and clear release notes that highlight the key changes. Use bullet points to list new features, improvements, and bug fixes.
- Highlight Benefits: Emphasize the benefits of the changes. Explain how new features and improvements enhance the user experience or solve existing issues.

Conclusion

Effective communication for Senior Developers involves the ability to present to both technical and non-technical audiences, collaborate across various functions, and write clear technical documentation, help guides, and release notes.

By mastering these communication skills, you can enhance your leadership, improve team collaboration, and ensure successful project delivery.

7: Staying Current with Technology

Introduction

It's mandatory to stay up-to-date with the latest trends and technologies, and to try anticipate trends and stay ahead of the curve. This session will cover strategies to help you remain at the forefront of technological advancements.

Strategies for Staying Up-to-Date

Continuous Learning and Professional Development

Online Courses and Tutorials

Online courses and tutorials are a great way to keep your skills sharp and learn new technologies, especially if there is an accredited certificate at the end of it!

- Follow Structured Learning Paths: Many online platforms provide structured learning paths for different technologies. Following these paths can give you a comprehensive understanding and help you progress from beginner to advanced levels.
-
- Certifications from reputable organizations (e.g., AWS Certified Solutions Architect, Google Cloud Professional Engineer) can demonstrate your expertise in specific technologies and keep you up-to-date with industry standards.

Books and eBooks

Books are a valuable resource for deepening your understanding of both fundamental concepts and new technologies.

- Read Technical Books: Invest in timeless technical books. Books written by industry leaders provide deep insights and best practices that can be applied in your work.
- Join a Technical Book Club: Meet with likeminded Readers and share your opinions and insights.
- Stay Updated with eBooks: eBooks are often updated more frequently than printed books. Subscribe to publishers or platforms that offer the latest eBooks on emerging technologies. Platforms like LeanPub allows you to read books *as they are being written.*

Networking and Community Engagement

Attend Conferences and Meetups

Conferences and meetups are excellent opportunities to learn about the latest trends and network with other professionals.

- Join Industry Conferences: Attend major industry conferences like AWS re:Invent, Google I/O, and Microsoft Build. These conferences often feature keynote sessions, technical deep dives, and hands-on labs.
- Participate in Local Meetups: Join or start local meetups and user groups related to your field. These gatherings provide a platform to share knowledge, discuss challenges, and learn from peers. They also can provide a new talent pool you can hire from when the moment arises.

Engage in Online Communities

Online communities and forums are valuable for staying informed and getting help with specific challenges.

- Join Developer Forums: Participate in forums like Stack Overflow, Reddit, and specialized tech forums. Engaging in discussions and asking questions can help you learn from others' experiences.
- Follow Industry Leaders: Follow thought leaders and influencers in the tech industry on platforms like Twitter and LinkedIn. They often share insights, articles, and updates about the latest trends and technologies.

Hands-On Practice and Experimentation

Personal Projects and Experiments

Working on personal projects is a practical way to apply new knowledge and explore new technologies.

- Build Side Projects: Create side projects that incorporate the latest technologies you're interested in. This hands-on experience is invaluable for understanding the practical applications and limitations of new tools.
- Experiment with New Tools: Set up a breakable-toy project or sandbox environment where you can safely experiment with new frameworks, libraries, and tools without affecting your main projects.

Open Source Contributions

Contributing to, or starting, open source projects is a great way to stay current and give back to the community.

- Find Relevant Projects: Look for open source projects that align with your interests and expertise. You can also just make your own. You'd be surprised how many people are trying to solve the same problems as you and who would love your knowledge!
- Collaborate with Other Developers: Contributing to open source allows you to work with developers from around the world. This collaboration can expose you to different approaches and ideas.

Staying Informed

Industry Blogs

- Follow Technical Blogs: Subscribe to blogs written by experts and organizations in your field. Blogs often provide insights into practical applications and emerging trends.

Podcasts

Listening to podcasts and attending webinars are convenient ways to learn while on the go.

- Listen to Tech Podcasts: Podcasts like "SpeakingSoftware", "Software Engineering Daily," "The Changelog," and "Syntax" offer discussions on current trends and interviews with industry experts.

Conclusion

Staying current with technology as a Senior Developer involves continuous learning, community engagement, hands-on practice, formal education, and staying informed through various channels. By incorporating these strategies into your routine, you can remain at the forefront of technological advancements and continue to grow in your career.

8: Outro / Wrapping Up

Introduction

Welcome to the end. Over the past sessions, we've covered essential topics that are pivotal for Senior Developers. In this conclusion, we will briefly revisit the key points we've discussed, reinforcing the knowledge you've gained and highlighting how you can apply these insights in your professional journey. Let's dive in!

Recap of Key Modules

2. Responsibilities of a Senior Developer

We began by exploring the multifaceted role of a Senior Developer. You learned about the importance of understanding business needs, translating them into technical specifications, and challenging requirements to ensure they are feasible and aligned with business goals. We discussed the significance of cross-functional collaboration and how mentoring and guiding junior team members through code reviews, planning sessions, and sharing resources contribute to a high-performing team.

3. Characteristics of a Successful Senior Developer

We then identified the key characteristics that define a successful Senior Developer. Effective communication skills, the ability to see the bigger picture, embracing change, and possessing a deep area of specialty were highlighted as crucial traits. These characteristics enable Senior Developers to lead teams, drive innovation, and solve complex problems efficiently.

4. Task Delivery for Senior Developers

Task delivery is critical to project success. We discussed planning and estimating projects accurately, prioritizing tasks, managing dependencies, and writing detailed RFCs or specs. These skills ensure that projects are well-organized, aligned with business objectives, and delivered on time, maintaining high standards of quality and performance.

5. Leading Small Teams for Senior Developers

Leading small teams involves effective task delegation, providing mentoring and guidance, and resolving conflicts. We covered the importance of regular check-ins, thorough code reviews, and fostering a collaborative environment through pair programming and peer feedback. Effective leadership ensures a cohesive, motivated, and productive team.

6. Communication for Senior Developers

Communication is a vital skill for Senior Developers. We discussed how to present to both technical and non-technical audiences, collaborate across various functions, and write clear technical documentation, help guides, and release notes. Mastering these communication skills enhances team collaboration, stakeholder engagement, and project success.

7. Staying Current with Technology for Senior Developers

Finally, we explored strategies for staying up-to-date with the latest trends and technologies. Continuous learning, networking, hands-on practice, formal education, and staying informed through various channels were emphasized. These strategies help Senior Developers remain at the forefront of technological advancements and continuously improve their skills.

Applying What You've Learned

As we conclude this course, it's important to reflect on how you can apply these insights in your daily work:

- Embrace Continuous Learning: Stay curious and proactive in learning new technologies and best practices. Dedicate time regularly to expand your knowledge and skills.

- Foster Collaboration: Actively engage with your team and cross-functional partners. Effective collaboration leads to better solutions and a more cohesive work environment.
- Lead with Confidence: Take on leadership roles with confidence, guiding your team through challenges and encouraging a supportive and innovative culture.
- Communicate Effectively: Practice clear and concise communication tailored to your audience, ensuring that everyone is aligned and informed.
- Mentor and Inspire: Share your knowledge and experience with junior team members, helping them grow and contribute to the team's success.
- Stay Adaptable: Embrace change and be open to new approaches and technologies. Adaptability is key to thriving in the dynamic field of software development.

Conclusion

The knowledge and skills you've gained here are crucial for your growth and success as a Senior Developer. By applying these insights, you can enhance your leadership, drive innovation, and contribute significantly to your team and organization. We wish you the best in your continued professional journey. Stay curious, keep collaborating, and keep pushing the boundaries of what you can achieve.

www.ingramcontent.com/pod-product-compliance
Lightning Source LLC
Chambersburg PA
CBHW071221240526
45470CB00018B/2193